100 Days
of Solitude

Andrew Mossford

Clink Street

London | New York

Published by Clink Street Publishing 2021

Copyright © 2021

First edition.

ISBNs:
978-1-913568-71-9 Paperback
978-1-913568-72-6 Ebook

I am delighted to have compiled these 100 poems, an intimate diary of my thoughts and observations through the most extraordinary of times.

Huge thanks to Jen for her support and creativity throughout (and for supplying me with the odd glass of wine as I sat blankly head in hands on the end of the sofa at midnight!).

To Cora, Kate, Annie, Prince and Bertie, for your boundless enthusiasm and positivity throughout.

To the Guest Poet – you know who you are!

To Mum, Claire and all my other family and friends, who's encouragement and messages throughout made it all so special.

Thanks to you all – we've been on quite a journey.

Day 1: Crappy Birthday, Annie!

Happy Birthday dear Annie, Happy Birthday my pet,
That sure was a Birthday, you'll never forget!
A raging pandemic; draconian rules,
Our futures uncertain, as you walked out of school.

Could be many months, til you're back there to learn,
Some of the children, may never return!
So terribly sad, makes you want to cry,
They barely had a chance to say 'Bye'!

The pubs have shut, the restaurants closed,
Not an easy decision, I don't suppose.
But Boris seems to be doing ok,
Growing into the role evermore each day.

The primary target, the current thrust,
Is to strike a balance between 'Order' and 'Trust'.
Sharing the responsibility and stress,
So we all support the NHS.

Just spoke to The Shanster, in New York City,
Things out there are none too pretty.
The healthcare seems to bypass the poor,
It could turn into a civil war.

Day 2: His Final Hand

Instructions today were that we should stop shopping,
As the masses can't stop the shop-to-shop hopping.
Our nation is struggling, of that there's no doubt,
As people just can't seem to stop going out!

A message that really is coming through strong,
Is the people who keep the world ticking along,
Are the supermarket staff; the delivery drivers;
And the healthcare workers, who so inspire us.

And what about the hidden force?
Who could that be? The teachers, of course.
Enabling key workers to work without tears,
By shielding their children from worry and fear.

Annie's Nintendo Switch has arrived,
To help with the endless hours inside.
And FIFA, the classic, her very first game,
Because life without football is quite insane.

And The Gambler played his final hand,
As Kenny Rogers departed our lands.
I'm sure that Dolly, will be shedding a tear,
So rest in peace to The Silver Beard.

Day 3: (Un)Mother's Day

"DON'T GO NEAR, YOUR MUM TODAY!"
What a horrible message, on Mother's Day.
They've brought us up, through all kinds of strife,
And our thanks are restricted to WhatsApp and Skype!

But it's not all bad, is what I'm finding,
'Cause every cloud has a silver lining.
Every day, face-to-face we speak,
Which beats a phone call once a week.

I spent most of the day scrubbing and cleaning,
Then strolled outside for some trampolining.
With dickie knees, and a dodgy back,
It's a miracle I managed to get off intact!

Then drove to Tesco, to give Kate a lift,
Our own 'key worker', who'd finished her shift.
The abuse she'd received, the customers to blame
The responsible few, should be ashamed.

Day 4: Lockdown!

At half-past eight, through gritted teeth,
Boris delivered, a momentous speech.
Unprecedented times, in so many ways,
We're now in Lockdown, for twenty-one days.

It could be longer, nobody knows,
Depends if the spread of the virus slows.
For the nation, this came as a bit of a shock,
We thought we were different – we're obviously not!

We had a fright of our own last night,
As Jen was sick, with all her might.
She's been feeling off colour for a couple of days,
But no other symptoms, now she feels ok.

And just before the nation closed up,
Mum dashed off to get her new pup.
They'll really be, so good for each other,
I'm truly relieved, and chuffed for my mother.

Day 5: The Arrival of Norbert

The very next day, after Mum got her dog,
We followed suit, and our's came along.
'Bertie' he's called, a real little treasure,
Holding a puppy is one of life's pleasures.

A little bit sooner than we'd had in our minds,
But the lockdown gives us, the perfect time.
What a fabulous way to pass the boredom,
Teaching Bertie to wee in the garden!

But 'Prince', the corgi, is not so enamoured,
Who is this creature, invading his manor?
"Oi, little fella, this is MY gaff!"
In a couple of days, they'll be having a laugh.

Our second 'key worker', gets up at half-five,
Off to Tesco, it's just a short drive.
An absolute dream, as they save all their dough,
They've nothing to spend it on, sitting at home.

It really is a bonkers thing,
When they get back home and need to get in.
Through the garage, they climb back in,
And chuck their clothes in the washing-bin!

Day 6: Weather, or Not?

Oh deary dear, it's hard to believe,
The irony isn't lost on me.
That after months of Biblical rain,
The sun has shown its face again.

But no, Oh no, Oh no-no-no!
Out in the sun, we cannot go.
Tantalising, a cruel twist of fate,
Like a carrot in front of the donkey's face!

To be honest, it's not just been overcast,
Relentless rain, it just wouldn't pass.
Terrible flooding, perpetually dark,
At one point, Noah went past in his Ark!

Some good news, it seems, for the self-employed,
Common sense has been deployed.
They may be inclined, to 'massage' their tax,
But it needs to be fair, and that's a fact.

Day 7: **Bless the NHS**

Happy Birthday to me! Happy Birthday to me!
Spent at home with the family.
Some lovely pressies, an Indian meal,
But this year, of course, it was not a big deal.

We got Mario Karts for the Nintendo Switch,
It doesn't half trigger my competitive itch.
Annie may only be 12 years old,
But I still love to ram her off Rainbow Road!

My 'working from home' is going ok,
It somehow has lengthened my working day.
But birthdays and work were put to one side,
The Main Event took place outside…

… At 8pm, we stood at our doors,
And joined, en masse, in a round of applause.
To all involved with the NHS,
Receiving your care, we are truly blessed.

You're as scared as us all, but you don't ever grumble,
Selflessly caring – I'm so very humble.
And so it transpired, in the calm, clear night,
The nation applauds you with all of its might.

Day 8: Covid v COBRA

Today the virus, bared its teeth,
Striking down our political chiefs.
First Boris, then Hancock, and now Chris Twitty,
This illness, is proving, to be quite… … indiscriminate!!

Did they follow social distancing rules?
Or did they feel, they were immune?
Yet no one deserves a Covid dose,
But Donald Trump must be pretty close!

'Virtual parties' are now all the rage,
On 'Zoom' or 'Houseparty', regardless of age.
Kate and her mates, dancing like wallies,
Alone in their rooms, each getting trolleyed.

And last night I was participating too,
Zooming in with 12 mates from school.
I loved it, just hearing the laughs and the roars,
Just like in the playground, in '84!

Day 9: Inevitability Knocks

There are new statistics, every day,
But one that struck me yesterday,
From the biggest cheese at the NHS,
Not mincing his words, a message to stress:

"If every one of us, stays inside,
No more than 20,000 will die!"
That really resonated with me,
A quarter of a jam-packed Wembley.

If all those people, stood two metres aside,
The line would stretch for 25 miles!
The inevitability that we all are faced,
Is we're not getting out of this one unscathed.

But we're in it now, so let's look ahead,
And do, just what, the experts have said.
Let's grab this virus by the horns,
Do what we're told, and STAY INDOORS!!

In years gone by, we'd be sent to war,
I know what I'd prefer, for sure.
No frozen trenches, or tin hats for us,
Just sit on the sofa, and don't make a fuss.

Day 10: Have I Had It? (Y/N)

One of the problems of Covid we've got,
Is whether you've had the damned thing or not?
The range of symptoms, continually prey,
On that psychosomatic part of our brains.

Jen's not sure if she's had a mild bout,
But no severe symptoms, have ever come out.
She's been sick, headachy, a little bit tired,
But no dry cough, or forehead on fire.

For a few of my friends, the diagnosis is tricky,
Like Chris at work, who was definitely icky,
And Ady, poor lad, was knocked out for days,
Cheltenham Races, where they caught their malaise.

With Cora and Kate, at Tesco each day,
The virus might not be that far away.
But at this stage, we're unaffected,
Unless it's in us, undetected!

Day 11: Pop-up Hospitals

A week and a half, I've been writing this verse,
But reality dawns, and it's quite perverse.
'Cause we think we've done well, to have not got
downhearted,
Truth be told, it's barely got started!

So far, at home, we're doing just fine,
Baking and cleaning and DIY.
In trying to fix, my broken jet-wash,
I almost blew my eyebrows off!

I sense the Government's started to find,
Its volume of testing has slipped way behind.
They're now playing catch-up, all hands on deck,
To build equipment, to test and to check.

And several buildings, voluminous in size,
Are being converted, into hospitals inside.
The G-Mex, Excel and the NEC,
They'll soon be full of those struggling to breathe.

Day 12: So Shall, M'Dear!

Even before Covid came along,
There were already signs that something was wrong.
Not so much how we're physically feeling,
More a decline in our mental well-being.

Perhaps it's not worse, we're just more aware,
Or is modern life just stripping us bare?
Beeping computers, long working hours,
Or is social media, sucking our powers?

I personally think, this isolation,
Will certainly worsen, the situation.
Although social media's, partly to blame,
It's also now vital, to keep us all sane.

The roads are empty, High Streets vacated,
But WhatsApp traffic, has escalated.
With Zoom and Skype and Instagram,
Let's use them all, as much as we can!!

Day 13: Numbers Game

The number of deaths took a nasty increase,
Up by 563.
And that's just in the U.K. alone,
It's now 50,000, across the globe!

It's always been something, that's intrigued me,
How naturally macabre us humans can be.
That inner devil, almost eager to see,
Just how high the final number will be.

In the US, the position is escalating,
The President's attitude, quite devastating.
I'm really not a political man,
But that bloody man's got blood on his hands!

On a positive 'note', Claire's keyboard's arrived,
(Dumped by the driver, halfway up my drive!)
My dad was a very, musical man,
Do his skills lie within, his No.1 Fan?

Day 14: The Cursed Child

Today, to Annie, my sympathies extend,
We're supposed to be down in London's West End.
To watch, the J. K. Rowling inspired,
Harry Potter & The Cursed Child.

We've waited for years to get our seats,
The tickets, she got as her Christmas treat.
The disappointment, she hid it well,
But inside, I'm sure, she felt cursed herself!

So Harry and Hagrid, will have to wait,
And Hermione, Ron and Professor Snape.
Instead, I wonder, what we'll watch at home,
Perhaps *Harry Potter & The Philosopher's Stone*?

The NHS's future improved,
Fourteen billion pounds, of debt's been removed.
And as the grateful nation, applauded key folk,
Dear Eddie Large, has told his last joke.

Day 15: Dear Dad

It's now 263 days,
Since you closed your eyes, and passed away.
But, oh my God, you'll never believe,
Just some of the things you would have seen…

The girls are still charming, hard-working and fun,
You really would be proud as punch.
And Jen still inspires the kids at her school,
So here, at home, we're all pretty cool.

Claire's going great guns, she just never stops,
And you'll never guess what – Mum's got a pup!
Dear little Nala, she's an absolute cracker,
Just like your Shelley, but a little bit blacker.

The footballing world, has gone quite perverse,
United are getting worse and worse,
City got banned, for continually cheating,
And The Reds have hardly ever been beaten!

I cycled the country, from bottom to top,
(You sure helped me beat the urges to stop!)
But in the last fortnight, I'm telling you, Dad,
The world's gone completely and utterly mad!!

A virus appeared, in a Chinese market,
'Bat soup', or something, is where it all started.
Now we're not allowed out, of the house for weeks,
And the queue for loo-roll, goes right down the street!

So you've done pretty well, to avoid all this,
Of course, you're still so terribly missed,
But your illness had dimmed, your shining light,
So perhaps, as ever, your timing was right.

Day 16: I (Don't) Think We're Alone Now

You'd be hard-pushed to say, I'm a 'handyman',
But there is a job, of which I'm a fan,
'JET-WASHING' – oh boy, oh boy!!
A truly wonderful, Big Boy's Toy!

Having fixed my jet-wash the other day,
Yesterday was time to play!
I jet-washed the patio, I jet-washed the path,
And in my break, I jet-washed the grass.

I jet-washed in all sorts of crazy places,
When people walked past, I jet-washed their faces.
I jet-washed the dogs, I jet-washed the cars,
I jet-washed my hands, and I jet-washed my arse!

And as evening came, we all went clubbing,
To 'Corona Club', where the vibe was buzzin'.
The kitchen transformed, just for the night,
With vinyl records and flashing lights.

Fair play to you, Cora, such enthusiasm,
And Jen, were you dancing, or having a spasm?
I'd say the 'Song of the Night' for me,
Was 'I Think We're Alone Now' by Tiffany.

Day 17: The Queen Speaks

I was proud to hear, the Queen tonight,
As her nation's in this dangerous plight.
Her family have often let her down,
But the Queen, majestically, wears the Crown.

The cynics, of course, will be spouting as ever,
But I'm of no doubt, it helps bring us together.
Yet why does the media ruin it all,
By releasing the content hours before?

I really do feel for the lovestruck teens,
Who in recent years, have striven to be,
Kissin' n cuddlin', in each other's arms,
It's such a shame, that they must stay apart.

It just makes you think, when this all stops,
When 'Loves Young Dreams', can again meet up,
When they put their romance, back into practice,
The Earth could well be knocked off its axis!!

Day 18: Boris & The Baked Potato

The dangers of Covid, are again laid bare,
As Boris is rushed to Intensive Care.
It's here. It's present. It's so realistic.
So come on, Boris, don't be a statistic!

Did he "Wash his hands, and stay indoors",
As The Baked Potato, does implore?
Matt Lucas's little, vegetable friend,
Perhaps a lot wiser than our own PM?

Every morning, at half-past six,
We get our hour-long, Chris Evans fix.
Alexa goes off, chronologically precise,
And the radio is on, as we open our eyes.

In times like these, uncertain and grey,
And it feels a bit like Groundhog Day,
People like Chris, so alive and upbeat,
An important fillip, as we get to our feet.

Day 19: Mother Nature Awakes

As the world has gradually, ground to a halt,
It's ever more clear that we're all at fault,
For taking our beautiful, planet for granted,
Have the seeds of recovery now been planted?

In not much more, than a couple of weeks,
A smile's come across Mother Nature's cheeks.
Her lungs are becoming pollution free,
And again she's loving to bathe in her sea.

So as the world struggles in despair,
Trillions of pounds have been plucked from the air.
So all this money – where the hell has it been,
As Mother Nature's been brought to her knees?

You'd like to think, now we're at the cusp,
That every single one of us,
All men and women, boys and girls,
Should all unite to save the world.

Yet can we rely on the powers that be?
I fear, maybe not, let's just wait and see.
But long after humans have wiped out each other,
It seems highly likely the Earth will recover.

Day 20: Family Life

A small saving grace of Covid 19,
Is something that's not been that recently seen.
That's having all of the family back,
Sharing our dinners and 'chewing the fat'.

We're taking turns to make the meal,
And the quality's really been quite surreal –
Magnifico pasta from Cora and Kate,
And 'meatball burgers' from Annie today!

It's been said before, but it's worth repeating,
Families sitting round the table eating,
Even just for once a day,
Can help in oh so many ways.

And the wider family, whom we cannot meet,
But now every day, we continue to speak.
So the virus is causing terrible strife,
But there are some pluses for family life.

Day 21: Puppy Love

Since I was just a little lad,
The thing I always wished I had,
The thing for which I yearned inside,
Was my very own dog to stay by my side.

Then when I was nearly thirty-three,
Along came The Major, and of course, Terry!
My beloved boys, such wonderful pups,
Worshipped us all, as the kids grew up.

In every photo, for so many years,
Their hairy faces would always appear.
They made me see what friendship should be,
Unconditional love and consistency.

Then Doggie Heaven came a-calling,
The hurt inside was quite appalling.
The hardest thing I've ever done,
Still haunts me now, two or three years on.

But although we'll never forget The Boys,
The house now sings to a different noise –
Prince and Bertie our new Best Friends,
They've certainly helped, our hearts to mend.

The joy they bring, to the family,
It's tangible. It's plain to see.
In times like these, as the horrors unfurl,
They take you away to another world.

Day 22: Good Fried Day

Crikey O'Reilly, it's Day 22!
We really seem, to be rattling through.
We're all conjuring up such things to do,
So I'm not all that bored yet – don't know about you?

In fact, I keep trying to keep aware,
And appreciate just how lucky we are.
We've got people, a garden and loads of pets,
Not banned from exercise – at least not yet!

Then Good Friday arrived – just like that!
To remind us again of a simple fact,
Being stuck inside, might not be top-notch,
But it beats getting crucified up on a cross.

The weather was oh so beltingly 'good'.
So hot I'd have jumped in the sea if I could.
The suntan lotion was dusted down,
So I didn't get third degree burns to my crown!

Then as evening fell, my heart missed a beat –
My childhood hero had got the disease.
No symptoms just yet, but still a worry,
So come on King Kenny get well in a hurry!

Day 23: Brave Hearts

At Thursday evening's round of applause,
Something happened that made me pause –
I had a little tear in my eye,
But I'm not quite sure exactly why?

We're thanking the nursing staff, of course,
But for me, I think, it's a little bit more.
It's not so much what they do for us all,
It's more why they started doing it at all.

I like to think I'm a reasonable bloke,
Works quite hard and enjoys a joke.
But doctors and nurses are different to me,
They work for others, so selflessly.

It must be in their genes when born,
When the 'caring' part of us is formed.
So it's not just gratitude that I'm feeling,
I admire the love, in their very being.

So come on, Suits, when Covid's behind us,
Don't ignore, with arrogant blindness,
The NHS is not a toy,
It's the nation's very pride and joy!

So the golden sunset on Thursday night,
Which, all in all, seemed very right.
As I banged my pan, I think that's why,
That little tear formed in my eye.

Day 24: DIY Scrubs

I wasn't alive in World War II,
But I kind of know, what we needed to do -
All those back home, just making stuff,
Stuff of which there wasn't enough.

And this behaviour, I'm seeing every day -
A friend of ours, Sophie, told us yesterday,
She's been doing some sewing, making hospital scrubs,
A noble effort, cause there just ain't enough!

And local schools have been showing great heart,
Teachers combining to play their part -
They've been using the hols to make some masks,
Doing their bit, without being asked.

To show just how mad are these times that we share,
Today Cora asked me to please cut her hair!
A 20-year-old girl, putting her style,
In the hands of a 'baldy' – now that's pretty wild!!

Day 25: Bernard the Dinosaur

A month ago, we raised a cheer,
For OAP Bernard, who did reappear.
No, he's not an old man, playing 'Hide & Seek',
He's our dear old tortoise, hibernating for weeks!

Our 60-year-old, three-legged mate,
Who back in November, curled up in a crate,
Closed his eyes, and gently exhaled,
Like Sleeping Beauty, with a face full of scales.

But now he's back, with his dandelion leaves!
Look deep in his eyes and it makes you feel,
Like the distant past, before you unfurls,
To a time when dinosaurs ruled the world.

It makes me laugh, how he's not got a clue
Of this virus-related hullabaloo.
He just crosses the lawn, up to the back door,
Opens his mouth, for dandelions, of course!

But not all of nature is so unaware,
And that's becoming loud and clear –
The morning birdsong's, received a tonic,
It's now like the London Philharmonic!

Day 26: Walkies!

For many years, I think maybe 15,
I've walked the dogs up and down the stream.
And it's hardly been busy on any day,
A bit like the stands at a City game!

But all of a sudden, things are changing,
The park now swarms, like a Lowry painting.
And all with dogs – but where had they been?
Surely not sat at home on settees?

Yet the social distancing rules have been made,
And for most of us they are being obeyed.
But the teens, they just can't seem to play ball,
Will we ever know the impact this caused?

And running again is back in vogue,
Pounding the miles along the road.
In the next Olympics if they ever take place,
The marathon's sure to be quite a race!

Day 27: Fake News

Thirty-one years ago, as of yesterday,
Hillsborough caused us such dismay.
Ninety-six fans sadly passed away,
Their families mourn to this very day.

An episode of such shocking proportions,
Showed the media's urge, for news distortion.
I abhor the newspapers' editor-chiefs,
Whose lies destroy lives, and they get off scot free.

And so to the virus, and how it's reported,
Are the facts and figures being distorted?
In times like these, you'd like to think not,
But a leopard never changes its spots.

Events like Hillsborough, and its aftermath,
Highlight the media's, chequered past.
You would hope, of course, that we'd learn our lesson,
But we don't, it's really so very depressing.

Day 28: "Tomorrow will be a good day"

Shortly after World War I,
A very proud Mum had a new-born son.
And that little boy went on to become,
The Nation's favourite, Captain Tom.

When we're all sat at home, feeling the blues,
Desperately yearning for a bit of good news,
Along came this spirited, genial man,
Who set himself, a bit of a plan.

He was planning to raise £1,000,
Circling his garden, round and round.
He reached his goal in about ten minutes!
But didn't stop there – this man wasn't finished!

Now I'm not the media's Fan #1,
But just this once, they are forgiven.
They used their power and influence,
To make an astounding difference.

By the time he'd done his 100th lap,
This World War veteran, in military cap.
Has raised for those nurses of whom we're so proud,
A breath-taking £15 million pounds!!

Now I'm not sure it's all about 'How much',
It's more the number of people it touched.
We salute you Tom, in these times we're apart,
You're safely entrenched in the Nation's hearts.

Day 29: When The Curtains Open

When this is all over (which could happen one day!)
The world will be different, or so they say.
But who are 'they', these supposed sages?
And realistically, what are the changes?

Of course, the economy will be flat on its back,
And we'll all feel the pinch as it slowly comes back.
And if any lessons have come home to roost,
The NHS will be given a boost.

But what about our society –
Will it truly change our priorities?
The 'key workers' who underpin the nation –
Will they now get true appreciation?

Will we remember what we mean by 'a school'?
"It's just for learning" – don't be a fool!
It's for nurture, support, a place to feel safe.
Not to be terrorised by the Ofsted State.

One thing's for sure, our hands will be clean.
Will we be kinder? That remains to be seen.
And one thing, I think, we'll all have found,
Is there won't be quite so much rushing around.

But as the curtains open, we won't all be there,
The family photos will be a little bit bare.
The tears will again, creep up in our eyes,
The tragedy being there were no Goodbyes.

Day 30: The Six O'Clock Beer

I run with the dog, two miles a day,
And yet my weight doesn't fall away.
An egg muffin there, an Easter Egg here,
Then at six I sit down and have a cold beer!

The government said we can exercise,
But the 'working from home' has caught me by surprise;
Ten hours a day – I'm up to my ears,
So at six I sit down, and have a cold beer!

When this is all over, some will be 'ripped',
And some people's diets may just have slipped!
Being the latter, I guess is my fear,
So at six I sit down, and enjoy a cold beer!

In times like this, it's a recognised fact,
That it's vital for us all to relax.
One of the ways to make my mind freer,
Is to sit down at six, and crack open a beer!

My legs are feeling 90 years old,
So in the shower, I touch my toes.
This also cleans my hairy rear,
So I treat myself, with a well-earned beer!

Day 31: A Short Month

It's hard to believe, that it's now been a month,
Since it felt the world was stripped of its fun.
For some, I know, the days don't half drag,
But for me, so far, it's not been too bad.

It reminds me a bit, of my bike ride last year,
When the end seems to never, ever, get near.
Mile after mile; hour after hour.
And mile after mile; and hour after hour.

But it's not that bad when you're going through it,
What could you do if you did want to quit?
Just ignore how far it is to the end,
Get your head down, and go round the next bend.

And the battle through this, it feels just the same;
Bit by bit, and day by day.
Just concentrate on the here and now,
And before you know, we'll be out and about.

So fill your day, with as much as you can,
Structure the hours, with a bit of a plan.
And while you think, how your day can be filled,
Captain Tom's on £26 mill!

Day 32: Joe King Inside

'Exercise', is the new golden chalice,
Our homes have become a Fitness Palace.
Getting fit on YouTube, is all the rage,
There's hundreds of choices, for any age.

Joe Wicks is by far the children's fave.
Joe Wicks is the one the housewives crave!
All lycra'd up, alone in their lounge,
With lippy and blusher in case he comes round!

I've even started to do some skipping,
But I guess you could call it 'elaborate tripping'!
Skipping, at my age – what a goon!
No doubt I'll be playing hopscotch soon.

When I knackered my back ten years ago,
The only things that helped the pain go,
Were Pilates and yoga – they saved my bacon,
Without them both, I'd still be broken.

So if I was King, of my very own land,
We'd all do yoga, every woman and man.
The money we'd save, for our NHS,
We would spend preventing a PPE mess!

Day 33: Mind Games

"Psychosomatic, addict, insane,"
As our friends, The Prodigy, did proclaim.
'Psychosomatic' – now there's a word,
Particularly apt in the current world.

It's when your mind goes a little bit mad,
Inventing an illness you'd never have had.
And with this current, invisible threat,
Your mind is playing tricks I'll bet!

A bead of sweat, upon your brow –
"Oh no, the virus has got me now!"
A tickly cough, a single sneeze –
"Oh no, I've got this dreadful disease!"

You've got a stiff back, and achy knees –
"Oh no, I've succumbed, to Covid-19!"
You couldn't taste, your chorizo stew –
"Oh no, I've caught this bloody flu!"

Day 34: Heaven on Earth

Fifty years ago to the day,
Was the very first of the World Earth Days.
Dreamt up by a Senator, and his chums,
The elaborately named Gaylord Nelson!

Now I'm not really sure what's been done today,
A little bit tricky when we're all locked away.
But the Earth's biggest enemy said "Look at me!"
As the Orange President planted a tree!

And tonight, just a few minutes after ten,
Just as the Earth is breathing again,
That infinite sky, so pure at dusk,
Defaced by the satellites of Elon Musk.

But today's not the day, for bad blood spillin',
Of these megalomaniac 'James Bond villains',
Today's the day, for us all to unite,
And Save the Earth, from its perilous plight.

Day 35: Heroes

So, St. George, today was your day,
But we have no more dragons for you to slay.
Our war is now against parasites,
And we need some Heroes to lead the fight.

We have Heroes who help us to survive,
When we're desperately fighting to stay alive.
The doctors and nurses, flogged to the bone,
Our only comfort, when we're scared and alone.

We have Heroes who help us to stay indoors,
Delivering everything, right to our doors.
And keeping the food distribution open,
Exposing themselves with little protection.

We have Heroes squirrelling away in their labs,
To find a cure or a life-saving jab.
We wish you scientists all the best,
If you don't win, will we ever rest?

'Heroism' is not an historical preserve,
St. George, for sure, may have "won his spurs,
In stories of old, all gallant and brave",
But we have true Heroes with us today.

Day 36: Escape to the Country

So we've already made it, to Day 36.
That's twelve threes, nine fours, or six times six!
Half a day's holiday for me today,
And I spent it wisely, I have to say.

With dear little Annie, clearing our brains,
Cycling through the Cheshire plains.
It's now seven months, since I sat on my bike,
And to get back on was really quite nice!

The towns are so quiet and I think I know why –
They're all zooming around the countryside!
Hundreds and hundreds of cyclists, of course,
And Boy Racer Terry's, with their noisy exhausts!

But in general, are people becoming more pleasant –
A friendly 'Hello' now replacing a grunt?
The North's not too bad, they've always been kind,
But are the Londoners closer behind?

So, yes, our ride was for exercise,
And, yes, the bonding was very nice.
But I'm just not sure why we loved it so much,
No doubt the countryside's magical touch.

Day 37: Pretty Pathetic

What the hell is Donald Trump?
A pretty despicable Orange Lump.
But what he's said now is beyond a joke,
It could be the death of some simple folk.

"Disinfectant obviously, kills the virus,
So go ahead, y'all, inject it inside us?!"
To appear super-clever, his insatiable thirst,
Well I'm happy to do it, if he goes first!

And closer to home, there's Priti Patel.
Is she taking the piss? It's hard to tell.
On national telly today she deduced,
The amount of shoplifting has reduced!

"No shit, Sherlock!" you bullying goon,
You'll inform us the Pope is Catholic soon!
How enlightening, sage and truly prophetic,
Thanks for that, Miss Pretty Pathetic.

Day 38: White Walkers

Personally, I'm not full of dread,
I've barely got a hair on my head.
But in a few months (three, maybe four),
Many of us will have visually transformed!

It may have seemed like the world has stopped,
But one's thing for sure, life has not –
And those little hairs upon our heads,
Are growing, and growing, into endless threads.

So when Lockdown's over, and the barriers are raised,
Out come the zombies, all sallow and grey.
Like a scene straight out of *Game of Thrones*,
White Walkers emerge in their haunting droves!

Like a *Harry Potter* fancy-dress ball,
When everyone comes as Dumbledore!
Or from *Macbeth*, the very first scene,
With thousands of witches, instead of just three!

The scrums outside the salons will be,
Like the most violent ever game of rugby.
So the richest people in the land,
Will be the hairdressers charging a grand!

Day 39: Chief Advocate

It's three weeks ago, since the nation paused,
As Boris entered the Intensive Care ward.
But now he's back at No.10,
Will he make the same mistakes again?

There's no denying, he splits the nation,
No universal adoration.
But Boris looked finished, or so we feared,
'Cause like him or not, that's a little bit weird.

His illness could be Heaven sent,
The NHS's defining moment.
'Cause underneath his pompous facade,
He must fight for the nurses, and bloody hard!

Shame on him if he lets it slip,
And succumbs to political one-upmanship.
He's not been behind the National Health, but
He should now be its Chief Advocate.

Day 40: Camp Garden

I don't want to bore you with Covid-speak,
But they seem to think we're at 'the peak'.
We're in the heart of the 'crucial days',
If we're going to avoid the 'Second Phase'.

The lockdown is almost yesterday's news,
There's a growing clamour to end it soon.
But come on now, let's show some patience,
To stop us all from becoming patients!

Annie wanted to camp, the other night,
In a tent in the garden, so I said "Alright."
Now let's not forget that camping is tough,
And under the moonlight, we sure had it rough:

Electrical hook-up; film on the tablet;
Goose-feather duvet; and cashmere blanket.
And when I woke up, desperate to pee,
I snuck inside, with the backdoor key!

Day 41: The Covid Generation

My heart goes out to the millions of children,
It could be September, til the schools reopen.
'Three months' for adults, is not that much time,
But for kids who are learning, it's like a lifetime.

But even 'learning' is not in first place,
It's more important that they are safe.
There's a lot of vulnerable kids out there,
And I'll bet, right now, a lot are scared.

And onto 'home schooling', which sounds so neat,
At least for a few days, or even a week.
Joe Wicks after breakfast; then maths for a pinch;
And arts & crafts – while dressed as The Grinch!

But the novelty, really, is quickly eroding,
I take my hat off to those still going.
Let's hope the children, don't suffer too much,
And Generation Covid escapes untouched.

So what lies ahead, for our kids and their friends?
Repeating the year? School at weekends?
But while we wait, to see what's to come –
'Happy 100th Birthday!' to 'Colonel' Tom!

Day 42: The Times They are a-Changin'

It's now pretty much six weeks ago,
When the madness began – we arrived back home.
With a plethora of grandiose schemes,
To achieve ourselves some lifelong dreams.

"I'm going to learn a foreign language."
"Well I'm going to clean out the flippin' garage."
"I'm going to do some DIY."
"And I'm gonna learn how to bake a pie."

Now six weeks on, I guess I can say,
There's not been that much progress made.
A concert pianist – that's what I'll be,
But I still can't even find middle C!

Now working from home, ain't all that bad,
I talk to Alexa, like someone gone mad.
"Alexa play that," "Alexa play this."
It's a really amazing bit of kit.

It reminds me of Oz, many years ago,
When I drove for three days, completely alone.
The singer of whom I never got bored,
Is the great Bob Dylan, the poetry lord.

Day 43: Repeat for a Week

Every weekday's exactly the same.
Not just 'similar' – they're exactly the same!
Every day. Repeat. Repeat.
Even my body knows when to excrete!

At 4am I'm bolt upright,
As Cora leaves in the middle of the night.
Then just before six – an ungodly time –
I hear, downstairs, the puppy whine.

So I let the dogs out for a wee and a poo,
Then back up to bed with a piping hot brew.
Finish the poem, then give it to Jen,
Who preps it for sending to family and friends.

At eight I go down and start to log on,
Enjoying my breakfast – a cinnamon bun!
I work for about ten hours to be fair,
(But I'm lucky to be working, so no complaints there).

Then off we go, for an evening run,
Back for dinner, then webcam with Mum.
Then Mario Karts, with Tim, Annie and Sally,
And finish the day with an hour of telly.
<Repeat for a week>

Day 44: Hello, Dear Son

Hello there, dear Son, I want you to know,
Thanks for your poem, a few weeks ago.
All good here but I have to say,
There are lots of people arriving these days.

At the Pearly Gates, the queues are so long,
St. Peter's struggling to cope with the throng.
By the looks on their faces they're all pretty scared,
I think they're a bit surprised to be here.

But we're making sure they're all ok,
And I have to say they're all very brave.
We're holding a quiz for them every night,
And the karaoke's, a right old sight!

But in my breaks, I have a look down,
To see what you're all getting up to now.
I saw your Mum, out walking her pup,
And is Claire really putting a greenhouse up!?

The girls still look like they're so full of fun,
And oh the smell of Jen's cinnamon buns!
I love that your house is so full of noise,
I laughed when you Zoomed with the Aylesbury Boys!

So keep on going, you're doing fine,
These really are extraordinary times.
If I see you soon, I'll be pretty mad,
But I'll see you again. Love, your Dad.

Day 45: I Am Jen

A momentous day for Bertie the pup,
On with his harness, once we'd all got up.
And onto the park, for his very first walk,
The smell; the sounds; if he only could talk!

I then did some of those 'Lockdown chores',
The type you'd never have got done before.
I gave the garage one hell of a clean,
And the bikes were all polished, and MoT'd.

Cora then cooked the most wonderful feast,
Roast pork, crackling and cheesy leeks.
And she had a theme that we'd all remember –
We'd each dress-up as a family member!

My task was to dress, as if I was Jen,
So I went in her wardrobe, like Mr Benn.
I chose an outfit true to her fashion,
A wig, nice dress, but the zip wouldn't fasten!

So we've come to the end of another day,
An intriguing day in many ways –
It started for me with Bertie inspired,
Then ended it dressed, like Mrs. Doubtfire!

Day 46: 'R': Sole Focus

So they want us to download an app on our phones,
To track where those with the virus go.
Call me 'Cynical Sid' if you like,
But they can go and take a bloody hike!

The lying, cheating, conniving gits,
Is there no end, to their sneaky tricks?
They might as well take the final step,
And stick a chip in our flippin' necks!

But it's all about, the magical 'R',
The favoured 'controlling measure' so far.
The most obsessed number the nation has watched,
Since Captain Tom and his charity pot!

So, if it stays at less than 1,
We should have Covid on the run.
But if the 'Co-vidiots' keep going out,
It'll go over 1, and we're all up the spout!

Day 47: Balancing Act

I sense that people have now had enough,
Getting out of Lockdown's all they can discuss.
But it's not going to happen, just like that,
It'll take many months to get it all back.

And the journey back is going to be weird,
Far worse, I suspect, than many have feared.
No groups, no pubs, no sporting events,
These things on which we all depend.

How d'you keep kids, apart at school?
To even try seems so very cruel.
And how will they keep office workers in check?
Will people sit at alternate desks?

It's such a precarious, balancing act.
The aged, of course, we must protect,
But when do the measures, that we must take,
Cause irreparable damage to the welfare state?

Day 48: The Beautiful Game

I've been writing these poems for 48 days,
And I have to say that I'm truly amazed,
That of all the subjects of which I've thought,
I don't think I've ever mentioned sport.

For almost my entire life,
Sport has been, my guiding light.
It's the reason I even know most of my friends,
And on it my conversations depend.

Golf, and triathlon, and squash, and lawn tennis,
And swimming, and cycling, and darts, and Real tennis.
But the one for me, that is miles above,
Is 'Football' – so clearly my sporting love.

I absolutely worship the sport,
The clubs, the players, and those who support.
'Jumpers for goalposts' is so very apt,
Its greatest trait, is 'simplicity' perhaps?

But when's The Beautiful Game back in play?
The speculation goes on every day.
And that's because it's a crucial part,
Of so many people – it's in their hearts.

Day 49: We'll Meet Again

It's a long time ago, since Dame Vera's lament,
So poignant, given recent events.
She mused about how 'We'll Meet Again',
But we've no idea 'where', and less idea 'when'!

They keep banging on, about the current crisis,
Comparing to when we defeated the Nazis.
But for me it's a totally different thing,
Psychologically, more than anything.

Is this war a foregone conclusion?
We expect a positive resolution.
It won't be pretty; it won't be brisk;
But is our future really at risk?

In World War II that wasn't the case,
Our future was often not looking great.
The nation had to come together,
Cause it really could have gone one way or t'other.

So that is why it's a Bank Holiday today,
To remind us of the sacrifices made.
We may be feeling freedom's gone away,
But our 'truest' freedom is not at stake.

Day 50: So What's New?

For 50 days, we've been living this life,
This crazy, crazy, messed-up life.
So what is different, or what have I done,
Purely because, the pandemic's begun…?

I would have met my mum's little pup,
But we wouldn't have had, our Zoom catch-ups.
I wouldn't have watched, the news every night,
Nor eaten a chicken Fray Bentos pie!

With Cora and Kate, I've spent much more time,
And even took Cora out on a bike-ride!
I've virtually disco'd, with the girls,
And was even let loose on Cora's curls!

I haven't watched any Sky Sports TV,
Nor even seen Liverpool win the League!
I've not even swum a single length,
The Channel in August!? Gimme strength!

I've not had the rush-hour drive me berserk,
Or worn my tracksuit-trousers to work!
I wouldn't have hidden in my desk drawers,
My very own secret chocolate hoard!

No daily runs, and I wouldn't have skipped,
Or heard of Captain Tom or Joe Wicks!
I wouldn't have written a poem every day,
Who knows how many more remain?

Day 51: German Germs

Jen and Annie's VE Day tea,
Was an absolute foodie masterpiece.
Carrot cake, sausage-rolls and cheese,
To commemorate the victory.

But it made me think of the Germans today,
In 'efficiency' they certainly lead the way.
But our countries, are of similar size,
So why is our death toll, more than five times?

Could it be London our capital city?
So big that the virus, could spread so quickly.
Or Cheltenham Races – should they have been stopped?
They seem to have been a viral hot-spot.

I suspect that the primary difference was 'testing'.
When you look at their actions – that's what's impressing.
Zey tested 'ere; Zey tested 'zer;
Zey tested bloody everyver!

Or maybe the answer, stares us in the face –
We're just a more irresponsible race?
Perhaps not a truth, that's readily admitted,
But make no mistake, I'd rather be British!

Day 52: 4 Out of 5

Oh dear, oh dear, all hell's broken loose!
It appears BoJo's update is of no use.
"Not enough," "Too vague," "His hair looks a mess!"
But what, on earth did you really expect?

We've proven we can't do as we're told,
So how can the government be remotely bold?
It feels to me like we still need a while,
'Cause give us an inch and we'll take a mile.

Now I've worked with numbers all my life,
And it gets my goat when they're not used right.
And now they've created this '1 to 5' score,
Well whoopie-do, we've scored a 4!

And another thing that gets my goat,
Are the bloody press – I'd stamp on their throats!
They raised people's hopes before tonight,
By spreading about, their mindless shite!

Now I looked in the mirror by accident,
And thought I looked like Prince Michael of Kent!
Not quite the image I'd like to portray,
So perhaps tomorrow I'll have a shave?!

Day 53: Frustration

Poor old Boris got a bashing today,
But fair enough, he was pretty vague.
No one was left with the faintest clue,
Of what they were now, allowed to do!

And again in the latest evening update,
His conviction, I would have said, wasn't that great.
Let's hope the experts, pulling the strings,
Are a bit more in charge of everything.

I'm delighted for Kate and Lorcan – 'her man',
They've been very mature throughout the ban.
We think they can now go and meet outside,
In each other's company, side by side.

So far in the crisis, I've been feeling ok,
But today has not been my favourite day.
Bit too frustrated to write a poem,
My creative juices are just not flowing.

Day 54: Back to School

I guess the topic of most debate,
Is when will they open up the school gates?
But what is behind the Government's haste,
To get parents to work – that could be the case?

It's a decision fraught with complications,
With very far-reaching implications.
Yet they've set a date of 1st of June,
Have they bitten off more than they can chew?

Is it the children's health at stake?
Not really, the risk is the teacher's fate.
They'll catch-up, I'm sure, with learning to read,
But for me, it's the 'socialising' they need.

But the kids will be prone to transmit the disease,
So hard to get them to "Wash your hands, please?"
And how do you keep the little ones apart?
They're five years old – what a difficult task.

So what are parents supposed to do,
Do they have to send their kids to school?
'Stay Alert' is the new message to keep,
Easy for parents – they're too stressed to sleep!

Day 55: Numbers Game

Today was National Numeracy Day,
And as I'm partial to number play,
I thought today's poem should contain,
A few of the numbers, around us today…

Let's start with a number, it's hard to digest,
33,200 deaths.
There's Covid-19 and 2020,
A 2% drop in the economy.

The target for R, is <1,
Five criteria, to gauge how we've done.
100,000 daily tests,
10,000 unexplained Care Home deaths.

51 days since Lockdown begun,
33 million for Captain Tom.
Bertie the pup, is 3 months of age,
You can now play golf with just 1 mate.

The weekly 8 o'clock round of applause,
24 hours a day indoors.
Zero trips to the hairdressers,
A million thanks to the NHS.

Day 56: The Great Return

I left the office at the end of March,
And thinking back, I was so in the dark.
I knew we wouldn't be back that soon,
Speculating, perhaps, the start of June?

But I certainly hadn't appreciated,
Just how the return is so complicated.
'All rocking up, on a Monday morn' -
That's just not how it will happen, for sure.

So who goes back first? And where will they sit?
They'll certainly have to stagger it.
And what about the furloughed members of staff?
How long is the furlough likely to last?

Childcare, of course, will play a big part,
In when we each are able to start.
Short-term carnage, but I do believe,
It'll all blow over, eventually.

Last night I went for a lengthy bike ride,
Through the gorgeous, sunny, countryside.
But I'm not as fit as I used to be,
It feels like someone's removed my knees!

Day 57: In the Headlights

I don't think I am completely alone,
In sensing a worrying undertone.
Has there really been, a bit of foul play,
In how the Care Homes, were squirrelled away?

Occasionally, when I watch the news,
I wonder who, are all these 'suits'.
The likes of Hancock, Raab and Shapp,
What a super bunch, of well-dressed chaps!

I'm sure they worked hard to get their degrees,
And schmoozed jolly hard to become MPs.
But where did they get the experience,
To make choices of such significance?

In many ways I feel sorry for them,
This massive pressure just dumped on them.
Up behind the lectern they stand,
Like startled rabbits, without a plan.

I really don't want to criticise,
'Cause these are such, extraordinary times.
But are they instilling faith and trust,
In a nation scared of going bust?

Day 58: The Invisible Threat

The virus is deadly, but let's not forget,
It's not the only invisible threat.
To some extent we'll all have felt,
The mounting threat to our mental health.

There's been greater awareness in recent years,
And much is now done to allay people's fears.
But after this, let's be realistic,
The problem's about to go truly ballistic!

Post-Traumatic Stress Disorder,
Is bound to be rife when this is all over.
The doctors and nurses – bless their souls,
To so many deaths they've been exposed.

It's human nature to want to be free,
It's not a 'desire', it's a basic need.
Which is why when we're all locked-up for so long,
That's a dangerous catalyst for things to go wrong.

But the modern world is hectic and stressed,
So there's quite a few people who feel more refreshed.
Free from the rigours of pressure and smog,
Enjoying the time with the ones that they love.

So if you're feeling a wee bit stressed,
The best thing to do is get it off your chest.
Awareness, really, is so much better,
Let's fight these troubles, and fight them together.

Day 59: Heart Attack Day

I thought today might be Heart Attack Day,
As I made my way to a freezing cold lake.
To start building-up my fitness again,
Open Water Swimming, my chosen event.

I've been wild swimming, many times before,
But I've worn a wetsuit to keep me warm.
But the purpose today was to make it tough,
So I did it, pretty much, in the buff!

With trepidation, I approached the start,
The cold, I feared, would shock my heart.
But I really shouldn't have worried at all,
My layer of fat, kept me toastie and warm!

For a minute or so, I felt a bit tight,
But it then became a total delight.
So refreshing and pure; such clarity of mind,
Away from all the chaos outside.

'Endorphins' I think, is how it's described –
They make you feel good, when you exercise.
And that's how I felt in that Cheshire mere,
Except that my 'meat and 2 veg' disappeared!

Day 60: After Extra Time

On Saturday, I was strangely eager,
To watch a bit of the Bundesliga.
The Germans, obviously, think it's safe,
We'll soon find out if that's the case.

I thought the game was pretty decent,
The players gave 100%.
But the total lack of atmosphere,
Made the whole thing extremely weird.

I'm sure they could add, the noise of the fans,
That can't be beyond the wit of man.
I'm intrigued to see if they make it work,
'Cause it could be a year, 'til the crowds return.

The powers that be, seem very keen,
To get the footy back on our screens.
They clearly see the benefits,
As so many people are missing it.

They say that footy's "Just a game",
But I'm not sure I agree, with 'They'.
Let's not underestimate its role,
In giving the country, a bit of its soul.

Day 61: Paw Salute

Last week we had, an emotional day,
'Cause a dear old friend had passed away.
For years we've walked, our dogs on the park,
But sadly he's now heard his final bark.

His send-off was lovely – a real touch of class,
As we all lined-up, along the path.
The hearse went past, with it's sad intention,
The dogs and their owners all stood to attention.

In the last few months so many have died,
Their families denied the chance to say "Bye".
But this was simple, and touching, of course,
The dogs even wept and raised a paw.

But time moves on, it never stops,
He and his wife, watched our kids grow up,
With seven dogs, we've shared our lives,
I cried on their shoulders, when Terry died.

I know I speak, for your friends on the park,
When I say your passing, has touched our hearts.
So keep looking down, and help me to see,
If that bloody dalmatian is off its lead!

Day 62: Sunny Flush

It was 'Thank a Teacher Day' today,
My god, who thinks up all these 'Days'?
But it's fair to cut the teachers some slack,
They really deserve a pat on the back.

One thing that's made this Lockdown better,
Is the beautiful, hot and sunny weather.
The boredom would be so much harder to bear,
If we couldn't go out and get some fresh air.

But day after day, the sun has shone,
It could be the carbon dioxide's gone?
No smog, no clouds, the sun beating through,
So Cora knocked up a barbecue!

An evening debut was good and bad,
Playing online poker with the lads.
Fourth hand; two-pair; I went all in -
A Crawshaw flush, and I was skint!

Day 63: Time Flies

Two months in, and to my surprise,
It feels like it's really flying by.
By now, I thought we'd have all gone mad,
But, for me, it just hasn't been like that.

The main reason being, I'm working long hours,
By the time I log off, I'm out of power.
So why then if I'm sitting all day,
Are my hunger levels off the scale?

But tonight after work, I took a break,
And swam 3k, in a coldish like,
(Perfectly socially distanced, of course!)
Then back for pizza and a round of applause.

Another interesting little spot,
Is the weather forecasts, have gone to pot.
They get their data, from commercial planes,
But of course, they're grounded – what a shame!

Day 64: Symptom Addicts

Oh how the pandemic plays tricks on the mind,
You think you're infected, but you're actually fine.
Every, single, little, twitch,
It's Panic Stations – "I'VE GOT IT!"

"I'm sweating a lot – is it Covid-19?"
Probably not, you had chillies for tea!
"I can't stop coughing – is an ambulance near?"
No surprise there, you inhaled a cigar!

"I cannot smell – have I got the disease?"
Well you don't smell very good, to me!
"My heart's achy breaky – I think it's the virus."
Who d'ya think you are – Billy Ray Cyrus?

They estimate one-in-four of you,
Have had the virus – most never knew.
So all those worries, that you're going to get it,
Chances are, you've already had it!

And good old Cora, she's at it again,
She organised Date Night for me and Jen.
An Italian feast, and bottle of wine,
"Grazie, Cora!" what a lovely time!

Day 65: Low Hygiene

In the 65 days we've been stuck at home,
I somehow doubt that I'm on my own,
In perhaps not washing as much as I can,
At times I've felt like Neanderthal Man!

Apart from my hands which I'm endlessly cleaning,
The rest of me just gets a monthly preening.
I really don't miss my morning shave,
I've saved a fortune on razor blades!

And I've also saved on the washing-machine –
Do your pants, every day, need to be that clean?
Stumbling-round at dawn, barely awake –
"These ones I've got on will last one more day!"

By the time my toenails need looking after,
They're like a bloody velociraptor's!
With them I could climb the face of the Eiger,
And tear the flesh off a sabre-toothed tiger!

So don't give up on your personal hygiene,
It's not just your hands, that need a clean.
'Cause walking around in a smelly bubble,
Could lead to future friendship troubles!

Day 66: Cummings Home to Roost

So who the hell is this Dominic Cummings?
And who the hell does he think he is?
BoJo leapt to his top aide's defence,
With a fair degree of belligerence.

The facts of the matter he was eschewing,
It made for quite uncomfortable viewing.
It's behaviour like this that appears so suss,
Is it one rule for them, and one for us?

While perusing on the internet,
Jen made note of the price of pets.
In the pandemic, one thing that's gone up,
Is the cost of buying a little pup.

But it's not just pups it's older pets too,
Their prices have just gone through the roof.
How bad must your financial worries get,
To be forced to sell your beloved pet?

Organiser-in-Chief was Annie last night,
As she put together a 'Ladies Night'.
Face masks, choccy, and a girly movie,
While the dogs played Mario Karts with me!

Day 67: Creative Truth

A proper pandemic – it's the best thing going,
To get those creative juices flowing.
Released from the hurly burly of life,
A time we may never, again see its like.

Annie's been painting, stones for the park,
And sewing a range of protective masks.
Kate has really come into her own,
Her art is special, her style all her own.

I don't know how Cora, dreams them all up –
'Corona Club'; 'Date Night'; and 'Dressed as us'!
Jen's been cooking, all sorts of cuisines,
Sourdough, her latest masterpiece.

And I've been writing a poem a day,
Who'd have believed I'd have so much to say!

And a man yesterday with plenty to say –
That Dominic Cummings, he ain't going away.
I'd like to forgive, in such trying times,
But it really sounds like a pack of lies.

Day 68: Furlough Vortex

The crisis has taught us a number of things,
One clear example, is this 'furlough' thing!
Where did it come from? What does it mean?
It's great when a word, just bursts on the scene...

The Yanks are sure, no strangers to this,
They're prone to jazz-up, their weather a bit.
A few years ago in the US North-West,
They had what they called, a 'Polar Vortex'!
Not a snowstorm; nor blizzard; or icy breeze;
A 'polar vortex', if you please!

But it's 'furlough' that I alluded to,
Defined as "grant a leave of absence to".
It's clearly helped us in the downturn,
But oh how we'll pay, in the longer term.
And despite its well-intentioned use,
I fear it's exposed to massive abuse.

Day 69: Guest Poet

It's been a real plus of this daily prose,
That some are inspired to give it a go.
So today's Guest Poet, is a friend from my youth,
It's over to you, Mr. A. Choir-Use…

Pain in my right leg, it's there all the time,
It gets worse 'n' worse, but the left leg's fine.
A cursory look, and with no hesitation,
"It's your sciatic nerve", was the doc's explanation.

I can't even walk to the end of Park Road,
The stairs are a struggle in any old abode.
So off to the physio, for a set of ten sessions,
My core improved, but the pain didn't lessen.

No footie with the boys, I can't swim, I can't run,
Can't cut my right toenails – oh what have I done?
A spinal specialist, I was sent to see,
What a waste of time that turned out to be!

He sent me for scans and injections galore,
MRIs, epidurals, spect scans. Are you sure?
I can't lace up my Sambas, it's like I've been cursed,
The virus took hold, I feel even worse!

Test results come back, "everything's just fine",
The smarmy twat says "it's not your spine".
But it's not 'just fine', I'm in constant pain,
But BUPA's paid you, your ill-gotten gains.

I'm advised to consult with Dr John Bull
Glad I called him, no bullshit at all.
Within 20 minutes, he'd set me straight,
"Why all the back tests, your hip's buggered mate!"

Steroid injection, is his short-term plan,
"A hip replacement, makes you feel a new man."
Dr Bull has, put both treatments on hold,
Hospitals full, some virus I'm told!

Day 70: Sea Dog

Wonders, it seems, will never cease,
And something's happened, you'll never believe,
We've had four dogs through thick and thin,
Now we've finally got one that can swim!

In the blazing sunshine, this afternoon,
Annie filled her paddling-pool.
And with the help of a blow-up croc,
Bertie 'The Sea Dog' – a wonderful shock!

And a couple of things, going round and round –
Firstly Cummings – how's he still around?
And every night, the Space Station hovers,
To tell the truth, I'm not really bothered.

I'm much more bothered that footy is back,
Which now it seems is becoming a fact.
The Reds are truly on the verge,
Of winning the Title they so deserve.

Day 71: Two Balls in the Sun

What a glorious day to be alive!
I finished work, at half-past five,
Popped in the garden – got a little bit burnt,
Then a round of golf with Terence Thorburn.

Golf really is a wonderful sport.
Some say "it ruins a jolly good walk",
But it's social, competitive and in the fresh air,
A temporary respite from worries and cares.

So it's back, it's back – golf is back!
Only two-balls for now, but we'll cope with that.
And it felt a bit odd, not shaking hands,
Just a tap of the putters, and nod of the heads.

The lifting of Lockdown, a bit suddenly,
Feels a little too quick, or is it just me?
I'm kind of onboard with this Track and Trace,
But I hear its weeks, 'til it's all in place.

Day 72: Thunder Pants

Today I got my certification,
From the Channel Swimmers Association.
Wearing goggles, a hat and a pair of pants,
I can now attempt to swim to France.

To qualify, what we had to do,
Was two hours nonstop, with no wetsuit.
A glorious day, but the water was brisk,
Cramp in my calves, was my biggest risk.

'Budgie Smugglers' are compulsory,
Unluckily for me, I didn't have any.
So Annie adapted a pair of my briefs,
No 'Best in Show' award for me!

The rules are quite officious, at best,
To copy the feats, of Captain Webb.
He was the first to complete the swim,
And now all attempts are an homage to him.

But I'm sure when he went, to buy his kit,
He was not in the midst, of a global pandemic!
And it was swimming Niagara, that later he died,
Yet his 'Health & Safety' rules still apply!

Day 73: Toilet Issue

So the Vulnerable millions can come out to play,
They'll protect their eyes, from the blinding rays.
But let's just hope they don't do too much,
This virus is very much still in touch.

But the end is really beginning to happen,
The economy's now got a bit too rotten.
And the acid test I do believe,
Is when will Social Distancing cease?

People from different families,
Can now meet in gardens, or so it seems.
But you can't go indoors, so what do you do,
If all of a sudden you need a poo?

Does that mean you must pack up and go home?
Or crouch round the greenhouse, all alone?
Or do you take your own little potty?
The journey home could be rather grotty!

It may seem as if, I'm being a bit flippant,
But the point I make is significant –
Until Social Distancing's gone away,
The world will remain a very strange place.

Day 74: Car v Bike

Kate passed her driving test six months ago,
Exactly how, we do not know!
But fair play to her, pass it she did,
And now she wants to get on with it.

But it's almost as if she's back to square one,
So this evening we went for a practice run.
A couple of stalls, but a decent drive,
No complaints 'cause we both survived!

It's a good time to practise, with so few cars,
But bikes are a bigger menace by far.
It's great to see them, out and about,
But they absolutely must watch out.

I love my cycling but I'm very aware,
Car v Bike? Only one winner there!
So please, please, please, if you're on a bike,
Respect the cars – don't risk your life!

Day 75: Cash War

It's a long time yet 'til the crisis is over,
And online shopping has taken over.
The Amazon Man has plenty of work,
Five times a day he drives Prince berserk!

Cash transmits the virus so well,
Its declining use is beginning to tell.
So with plastic cards and online shopping,
The future for cash could be very choppy.

Oxfam will open in a day or so,
They'll be PPE'd from head to toe.
But the teachers are back to their teaching today,
With no PPE – what a slap in the face!

And America's problems are beginning to steeple,
Trump is waging war on his people.
We always suspected he'd start a war,
But not within his very own shores!

Day 76: Timber!

Guess who we had round today?
Three young lumberjacks, and they were OK!
We had a 60-foot tree chopped-down,
The neighbours wore their customary frowns.

To be fair they did make quite a racket,
But the tree was rotten – it had totally had it.
Prince and Bertie were none too pleased,
At the Chainsaw Massacre in the trees!

After days of sun, we've now had some rain,
I hope we don't see a new Spike of Pain.
We know the virus transmits better indoors,
So we'll have to be extra careful, of course.

But the risk of a spike is even higher,
As the massed protestors vent their ire,
At the sickening events in the USA,
Let's hope our efforts don't go to waste.

Day 77: Animal Crackers

This crisis could really change the nation,
There's bound to be some devastation.
Despite the Government's payouts and grants,
Plenty of businesses will not last.

But it's not just businesses that could struggle,
Some places we love are also in trouble.
Sports teams, pubs and theatres too,
And today's cry for help, from Chester Zoo.

Will the impact really, be so severe,
That places like Chester Zoo disappear?
Places to roam, to enjoy and to rest,
When lockdown's relaxed, what will be left?

Sometimes I feel it's all just a blip,
It'll all blow over, and pretty quick.
Then sometimes I fear it could go on,
And on. And on. For so very long.

I've just re-read what I've said today,
And it's not very positive, I have to say.
But a bit of good news is coming our way,
We'll see my sister and Mum in two days!

Day 78: NO CAMPING

I really felt like a git yesterday,
An officious, nauseating, bloody pain!
'Cause Kate and her boyfriend wanted to stay,
In a tent in the garden, for just one day.

They've been so good through this chaos so far,
Obeying the rules and keeping apart.
Then all they want is to sit in a tent,
But the Big Bad Git says, "No you can't!"

I have to say I didn't feel great,
Having to kibosh their canvas date.
But lots of people have made no fuss,
When they've sacrificed far more than us.

To be fair, they totally understood,
Putting on a brave face, as best they could.
So we turned on the telly, a little downhearted,
And would you believe, The News had just started.

And what we saw didn't help matters,
On beaches, in parks, people were scattered.
Shoulder-to-shoulder, hips-to-hips,
The virus must have been licking its lips!

It's moments like this, that make me worry,
This crisis won't be gone in a hurry.
Even those that are doing their bit,
Need the support of the Big Bad Git!

Day 79: Same New World

It seems that the virus, is now on the slide,
(These political protests, put to one side!)
So once we've seen the back of this,
There's quite a few things I'm going to miss...

I won't miss the stress of the daily commute,
I've loved the time in my favourite tracksuit,
Cora and Kate, back home and so chipper,
And all sat round for our family supper.

And speaking to family and friends so much,
And I've not spent any money for months!
Our communal respect for the real 'key workers',
And people just seem to be nice to each other.

The Simplicity of Life, has been a big plus,
I've mentally had a timely adjust.
I've enjoyed being free from organising,
Like booking hols and all sorts of things.

So will the New World revert back to type?
It became how it was 'cause that's what we're like.
I suspect it will (I've been around too long!)
But oh my god, I hope I'm wrong.

Day 80: Sausage Fest

Early this morning, we jumped in the car,
And made our way to Leamington Spa.
It was lovely to see Mum and Claire again,
And also our good friends, Sally and Ben.

But the humans, did not take centre stage,
As we all had puppies of about the same age.
But the similarities didn't end there,
They're all mini-dachshunds with different hair.

There's long-haired Nala, so pretty and petite,
And short-haired Daphne, so smooth and sleek.
And wire-haired Bertie, all moustache and winks,
And the Hugh Hefner figure, our corgi Prince!

We all got our pups on about the same day,
Just as the lockdown came into place.
And stuck in our homes we all agree,
They've been amazing company.

So gridlock in Leamington Spa today,
As the sausage dogs came out to play.
But 'sausage' might be being too kind,
'Chipolatas' more what springs to mind!

Day 81: Rhyme Time

I've been going for over 80 days,
And sometimes I struggle to find things to say.
So hope you don't mind if just this one time,
I indulge myself with some crazy rhymes…

I wonder how many people called Klaus,
Have sneezed in the Sydney Opera House?
And my favourite drink is orange squash,
Mixed with joy by Hugo Boss.

Timmy Taylor's soldier's pies,
Are shaped like the Sultan of Brunei.
And you'll always want to chew rhubarb,
When you're on a factory tour of Saab.

Elizabeth Fry and John Paul Getty,
One called 'Betty', the other a yeti.
And I once bought a Pringle cardigan,
That came with a single Tommy gun.

My terry towelling tight pyjamas,
Subtly smell of the Dalai Lama.
And Prince's favourite colour was purple,
But I doubt he wrote a song called 'Gurple'.

Day 82: Hidden Trauma

It was way back on March 17th,
When Sir Patrick Vallance did decree,
If less than 20,000 die,
He really would be quite surprised.

I remember my shock at what he'd said,
Expecting so many people dead.
But we had no idea of the mounting trouble,
The death-toll's shot up to more than double.

If each of the 40,000 deceased,
Had 25 friends and family each.
That's a million people, emotionally wrecked,
With long-lasting issues, I would suspect.

So 40,000, yes it detests,
But what about, the knock-on effects?
Since that decree on 17th March,
More than you think have aching hearts.

Day 83: Birthday Balderdash

It was Lockdown Birthday Number Three,
As dear old Kate did turn 19.
Cora chose an Hawaiian theme,
As Jen made steak & chips for tea.

And what a Birthday gift she got,
As the Government pulled out all the stops.
It seems that she could be allowed,
To see more of her boyfriend now.

Then after dinner, we decided to play,
'Balderdash' – the best board game.
A game of creativity and riddles,
But better than that, an absolute giggle!

Today they made note on the Evening News,
Of the other elephant in the room.
Raise your hand, and raise it high,
If Brexit seems to have passed you by.

But I believe it might still be going ahead,
'Deal' or No Deal' or whatever they said.
Such a massive thing that reaches so far,
Stealthily approaches, under radar.

Day 84: Who are the Lucky Ones?

One of the most important things,
That people seem to be really missing,
Is getting away for weekend breaks,
And of course, our summer holidays.

And because we can hardly go anywhere,
It's hard to use up your holiday share.
I've hardly had a day off this year,
And I'm starting to feel a little bit weary.

But I still feel very fortunate,
Although it means I'm working late.
And I've less spare time than I had before,
It beats the alternative, that's for sure.

I thought this 'furlough' would be interesting,
I could draw and get fit (but not learn to sing!)
For a while the freedom would be very real,
But it might not take long to lose its appeal.

My friends on furlough have had enough,
Most are now finding it pretty tough.
The uncertainty, worry, is now running deep,
With more time to sleep, they struggle to sleep!

Day 85: First Trip to London

This morning, I'm off for a bracing swim,
So again the Guest Poet, is stepping in…

First trip to London since lockdown began,
For an injection, from a medical man.
The green and white shape of the Southern Train,
Oh what a surprise, it's late again!

Rush hour's passed, I'm on the 10.53,
There's loads of space, it's nearly empty.
Familiar sounds, and familiar sights,
Past Box Park School and the Selhurst Park lights.

Getting off the train is a simple task
But I nearly forgot to put on my mask.
I go down the stairs onto the concourse,
The one-way systems are being enforced.

I select a seat and look all around,
People are wary, and masks abound.
Phones being checked, no coughs nor a sneeze,
But I'm left with a feeling of great unease.

This type of feeling I'm trying to recall,
Has he got it? Or her? Or anyone at all?
Not bombs but the virus, that's a threat to life,
This feeling is similar to 2005.

Day 86: Benchmark Year

Throughout the annals of history,
There's been moments of terrible infamy.
Events of such notoriety,
They serve to benchmark our memories.

World War II and its six years of hell,
Before most of our times, but we know it so well.
In the 60s there were the violent killings,
Of Kennedy and Martin Luther King.

Then the horrors of 1986,
Chernobyl and Challenger – blown to bits.
In 97, poor Diana succumbed,
And the Twin Towers felled in 2001.

So are we experiencing, the biggest yet?
The year 2020 – we'll never forget.
Perhaps not for, the number of deaths,
More for the longer-lasting effects.

Day 87: Support Trouble

So another weekend, simply whistles by,
Just as they did, in normal times.
We've got one new ruling causing all sorts of trouble,
What on Earth do they mean, by a 'Support Bubble'?

Did a five-mile swim on Saturday morn,
And into the water so many poured.
After such a prolonged exercise drought,
Good to see people, getting out and about.

But as ever there's always the 'Doughnut Brigade',
Like the brainless pricks and their Quarantine Rave.
And I'm not so sure what the police did so wrong,
To be battered in London by a sweaty throng!

For normal shops, the rules are relaxed,
'Guard of Honour' for me, at TK Maxx!
And now there's only three days to go,
To the grand return of the Premier League show!

Day 88: The Drone Collector

My old mate Tim is a techno junkie,
And his latest gadget is pretty funky.
He's bought himself a Lockdown pressie,
It's called a 'drone' and it's very impressive.

We were treated to a little demo,
Out in the heart of a countryside meadow.
Dodging the cowpats and clouds of pollen,
Up rose the drone, like a Roman column.

With its onboard camera, snooping around,
Nothing was sacred, as it looked on down.
And the mini-Airwolf could fly far away,
It can still be controlled ten kilometres away!

What a truly fabulous bit of kit,
It has sensors, can balance, and all sorts of bits.
All controlled by Timothy's phone,
The future's bright. The future's a drone.

Day 89: Steroid of Use

I caught a glimpse of The News tonight,
And the headline gave me a pleasant surprise.
It seems that some steroids just might help,
To cure Covid victims with declining health.

I can't quite remember its fancy name,
Something like 'Dexys-midnight-methane'?
Or 'Dexter-me-and-some-old-jerk'?
Oh, who bloody cares – as long as it works!

And oh what a difference it could make,
To put Social Distancing in its place.
'Cause until Social Distancing is relaxed,
We'll never get our normal lives back.

And Marcus Rashford has used his position,
To ensure that kids get enough nutrition.
Now I'm certainly not a United fan,
But fair play to Marcus – well played, young man!

Day 90: Football's Come Home

It's back! It's back! Football is back!
To the football authorities – a pat on the back.
It has to be said it was a bit weird,
Just, I suspect, as we all had feared.

Sheffield United made a trip to the Villa,
But the game was certainly not a thriller.
As ever, technology stole the scene,
As Hawk-Eye missed what we all could see.

Apart from, perhaps on my Asian Adventure,
My life's had footy, right at its centre.
And I know there are months between each season,
But this delay had abnormal reasons.

So I'm glad that it's back – but why so soon?
For the fans? Or just to crown Liverpool?
To dilute society's acrimony?
I think we all know, it was just down to money.

Day 91: Test of Pride

Lockdown, for me, has been pretty nonstop,
From one thing to another, all round the clock.
So I'm treating myself to three days off,
But my tennis and golf got bloody rained-off!

So we spent the morning driving round Cheshire,
Free from all the daily pressure.
Checking out houses that we just might target,
And take a punt on the housing market.

Then I settled myself down for a bit of TV,
Curled up on the sofa with Prince and Bertie.
Fire in Babylon was just the ticket,
A great documentary, all about cricket.

Now cricket is not a game I exhort,
But this film is about far more than sport.
If you've never seen it, then really you ought,
About the West Indies and the battles they've fought.

The racist abuse from the Aussies and Poms,
So shameful. So hurtful. So totally wrong.
And still so pertinent, in current times,
An inspiring team, exploding with pride!

Day 92: Goodnight Sweetheart

In the last three months, so many have perished,
Each of them loved; each of them cherished.
They'll all be missed, of that there's no doubt,
So it seems a bit churlish to single one out.

But there is one exception who loved to sing,
'The Forces' Sweetheart', Dame Vera Lynn.
Having lit the hearts, of those brave young men,
True to her word, she's just met them again.

And on a completely different tack,
What's this I hear, of a cyber attack?
An attempt to hijack the Aussies' income –
"Strewth, that's not very nice, fair dinkum!"

First we had Brexit – the abomination.
Then Covid-19 and it's devastation.
Can you just imagine if we followed all that,
With a full-blown global cyber attack?

To be honest, I'm not really sure what would happen,
Our techno network, I suspect, would be flattened.
Our phones are now such a part of us,
If they all went off there'd be utter chaos!

Day 93: Remember Father's Day

It's Father's Day, Hip-Hip Hooray!
A day for all to celebrate,
How much they love their dear old Dad,
Recalling all the times they've had.

But some can't see their Dad at the mo,
Can't even pop round to say 'Hello'!
And others whose Dads, are terribly missed,
Particularly at times like this.

I've been on this planet for 49 years,
And this is the first when my Dad's not been here.
It's nearly a year and he's still sorely missed,
But I think he's done well to escape all this.

Dementia had swallowed him into its claws,
With most of the onus on Mum, of course.
If he'd still needed care through all this mess,
The only outcome – heart-breaking distress.

But there's still so many in need of care,
My heart goes out to the carers out there.
You may think that Lockdown's not been good for you,
But dementia carers – we all salute you!

Day 94: Universal Harmony

They're still pouring through the Gates up here,
We've had nearly half a million appear.
On the whole, I guess, they're all pretty old,
And they've certainly come from all over the world.

The Chinese came first, then Italians,
Followed by quite a few Europeans.
The Yanks and Brits then filled the next wave,
And India and Brazil in more recent days.

A wide-ranging mix, of all races and creeds,
And as we look down, we all agree,
That the prejudices – so abundant down there,
Have all disappeared when you come up here.

Human nature has a self-destruct button,
By driving wedges between one another,
But up here that really isn't the case,
This truly is a harmonious place.

Day 95: Pollen Daze

So to the end of my three days off,
And this time the pouring rain held off.
A lovely walk with Prince & The Pup,
But boy, my hay fever's playing up.

The clouds of pollen swirl in the breeze.
So if I had the virus, and let out a sneeze,
And if it was one of my Sunday best,
I'd probably infect the whole North West!

That said, the North West ain't doing too great,
It appears to have the highest R-rate.
It's all so very disappointing,
The apathy for distancing.

And 'The World's Greatest Covid-busters' themselves –
Has the Germans' discipline also been shelved?
It seems they now, have a spiking R,
"Das ist nicht, so wunderbar!"

And Trump continues to spout his s#!t,
"Kung Flu" his latest inflammatory quip.
It's hard to know whether to laugh or cry,
What a truly toxic Master of Lies.

Day 96: Four Grand

My word I'm getting itchy feet,
To get away, even just for a week.
And I don't even want to go abroad,
Just Scotland, The Lakes or the Norfolk Broads.

I'm not too fussed about luxury,
Fancy hotels are just not me.
I'm an outdoor loving, simple man,
And I've got an urge for a campervan!

How much do they cost? So to get a flavour,
I took a quick peek, in the Autotrader.
£3-9-9-5? Or call it four grand?
But I soon found out they're far more than I'd
planned!

So now I must think about a Plan B.
I'd still like to go somewhere near the sea,
But instead of a van with its own private loo,
Perhaps it's a tent with an outside poo?

And it's not just me, who wants away –
The Government Updates that they've done
every day,
Have been scrapped by BoJo and his friends,
A very clear sign that we're nearer the end.

Day 97: Come On, Vaccine

Taking part in a vaccine trial,
Not for me in a million miles!
It's such a selfless thing to do,
So those who do it, fair play to you.

A Covid vaccine – what a massive prize,
That's why some are happy to risk their lives.
How on Earth do these trials even work?
Just pop a pill – then you might go berserk?

I believe, in Oxford, a vaccine's been made,
But it takes so long, to get the 'ok'.
I suppose the risks in this case are clear,
If they get it wrong we could all disappear!

And the weather's gone, all scorchio again,
The hottest June day there's ever been?
The only thing hotter anywhere,
Are the Anfield Reds – they're nearly there!

Day 98: Covid-19th

Annie was back footy training last night,
And it really was a heart-warming sight.
Back with their mates, after all those weeks,
The sun beating down; smiling cheek to cheek.

Understandably what they could do was restricted,
No matches or shooting – adhered to strictly.
Difficult rules for the coaches to preach,
As millions flocked to a Dorset beach!

But that was not yesterday's big football story,
As Liverpool FC were bathed in glory.
After 30 long years, they've won the League,
Back on the perch where they've longed to be.

An historic win, for so many reasons –
Just seven points dropped, an astonishing season.
With a three-month Covid wedge through it,
And the fear that the 'Powers that be' would scrap it.

But after all, common sense prevailed,
The Anfield Reds have their Holy Grail.
After 30 years and some extra weeks,
The tears could finally, run down their cheeks.

Day 99: Good & Bad

Although the crisis will rumble on,
It really seems that the worst is gone.
So as a country looking back,
How've we handled the virus attack?

For sure, the Government made some gaffes,
With a lack of PPE and masks.
You can forgive them, their honest errors,
But have they hidden, some Care Home terrors?

Each country's taken a different approach,
But who's course of action has saved the most?
For me it's a futile numbers game,
Played by those wanting someone to blame.

But one thing I know for certainty,
It's far from over for some countries.
You fear for the less-developed nations,
And in the States, it's escalating.

I've always been proud of our little land,
Our diverse mix of woman and man.
Freedom of spirit which sometimes obstructs,
But on the whole is a massive plus.

Day 100: 100 Days of Solitude

Well here we are, the time has come,
To write my final, Covid poem.
And I'd like to end with a summary,
Of what the crisis meant to me.
Just like the diaries of little Anne Frank,
I've tried to be open, honest, and frank.
And what a hundred days it's been,
Surely the strangest, we've ever seen.

'Gratitude' I think, is my main emotion,
I've felt quite removed from all the commotion.
I've not been stuck in a flat all day,
With stir crazy kids just wanting to play.
It's been great to have the family back,
And Prince & Bertie to make us laugh.
And although the virus has taken so many,
I'm thankful that I don't know of any.

When all this began I had grandiose plans,
Like art and becoming a slimmer man!
But now it feels with the virus going,
All I've achieved is 100 poems!

I'm extremely proud of my family and friends,
And how on each other, we all depend.
As the saying goes, we're like 'birds of a feather',
It's brought us all even closer together.

But I'm less upbeat about what comes next,
What does this mean for our future prospects?
When the vaccine's ready, and economy's returned,

Do you really think there'll be lessons learned?
Personally I think 'Not a Chance',
We'll just revert to the same old dance.
The blinkered views of short-termism,
Is how the modern world is driven.

I've been very touched by the comments I've had,
So I'd like to say, a big 'Thank You' for that.
And as much as it gave you all something to read,
It was also therapeutic for me.
It made me think what I really think,
About so many different things.
I might write some more if things get worse,
So let's hope this is my final verse!
The end of my chronicle of Covid views,
In '100 Days of Solitude'.

Lightning Source UK Ltd.
Milton Keynes UK
UKHW040240081021
391819UK00002BA/324